World Faiths Today Series

Exploring the Paris

**Who are your friends? Do you k...
them? Do they know everything**

Well, this is a story about friends who do... about one another. But they are starting t... ...some things their friends do and why they do them. Read their story and you might learn something new too!

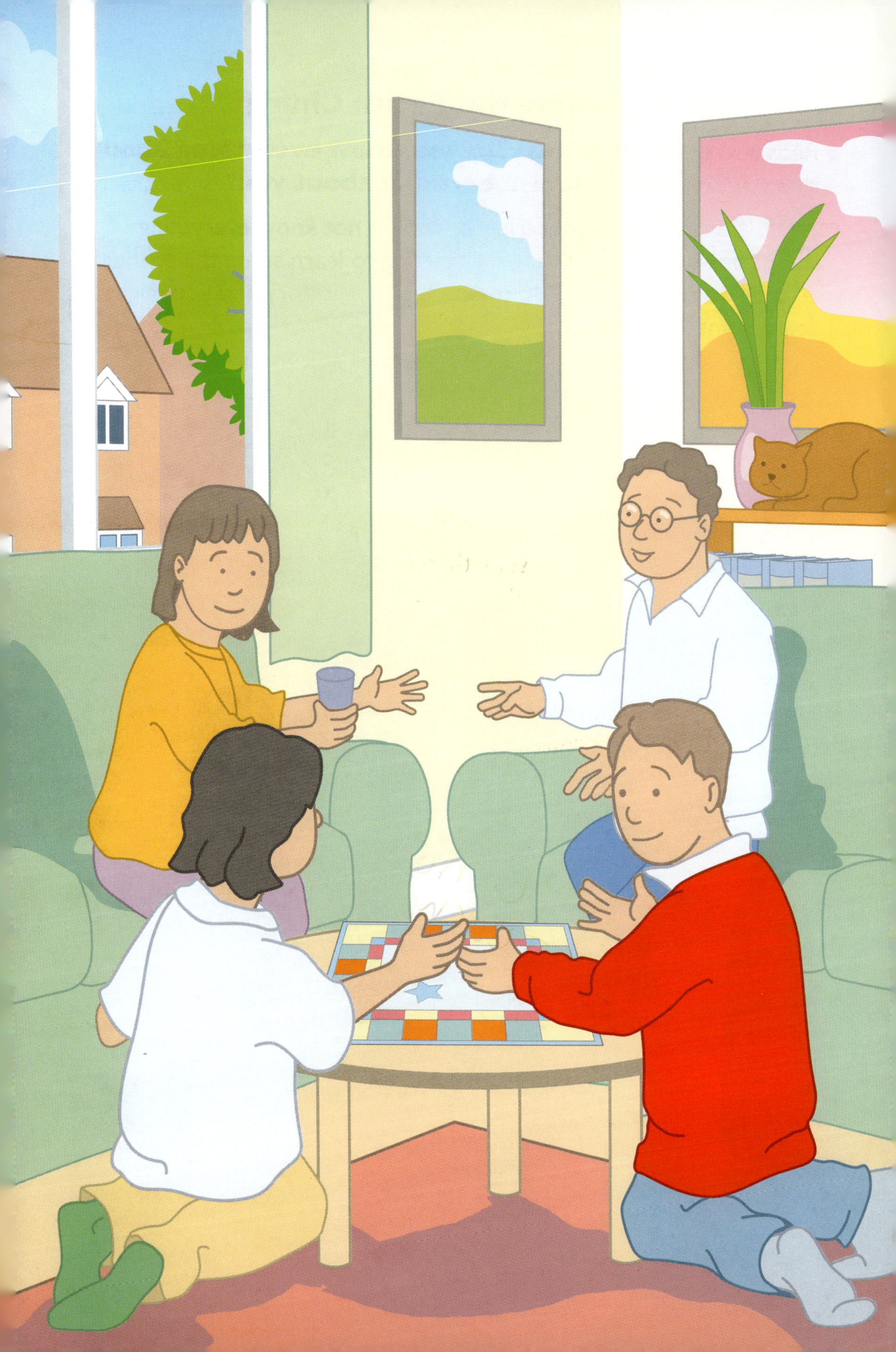

1 Visiting the parish church

Rees and Sara had got to know Bethan and Tomos quite well since they had moved into the house next door a couple of years earlier. They would visit each others' homes to play and sometimes stay for tea. Occasionally they even had sleepovers, which were a lot of fun.

Bethan and Tomos' father worked in the local high school as a science teacher. Their mother worked as the priest in the local parish church, St David's. They were a Christian family.

Bethan and Tomos' mother, Mrs Davies, often dressed differently from most other mothers. She wore special clothes to show that she was a priest. Sometimes she wore a white clerical collar with a smart black shirt, or with a more colourful shirt. Sometimes she even wore a long black cassock that went all the way down to the ground. Rees and Sara wondered how she managed never to trip over the hem.

On this particular Sunday morning, Rees and Sara were dressed in their very best clothes. Tomos and Bethan had invited them to a service at St David's Church.

It was a very special Sunday for Bethan and Tomos because they were going to receive communion for the first time.

'We have been going to church on a Sunday ever since we were babies,' Bethan told Sara. 'Now today we are being invited to receive communion for the first time.'

'We have followed a course of preparation,' added Tomos. 'Now we are ready to take a full part in the life of our church.'

Sara and Rees were proud to share in their friends' special day. When they arrived at church, Rees and Sara sat in a pew with Bethan and Tomos and with Mr Davies.

The children sat very still and listened to the organ music.

When the organ music stopped, everyone stood up to sing the first hymn. During the hymn, Rees and Sara gazed in wonder at the procession of the choir and clergy.

The procession was led by the crucifier carrying a tall cross. Just behind the cross, the two acolytes were carrying processional candles. They were wearing long white albs. Then came the choir of boys and girls, men and women, all wearing white surplices over long black cassocks. After the choir came the reader wearing a white surplice and blue scarf. At the very end of the procession came Mrs Davies. Mrs Davies was wearing a green chasuble, showing that she was going to lead the communion service.

Mrs Davies took her place behind the altar. A man and a woman from the congregation read two lessons from the Bible. Mrs Davies read a special passage from the Gospel according to St Mark. Then, the reader preached the sermon.

Rees and Sara watched as some children from the congregation carefully carried a dish of bread, a jug of wine and a jug of water to the altar. Mrs Davies placed the bread on the altar and said,
>'Blessed are you Lord God, King of the universe.
>By your goodness we have this bread to offer.'

Mrs Davies poured the wine into a silver chalice and mixed with it some water. She said,
>'Blessed are you Lord God, King of the universe.
>By your goodness we have this wine to offer.'

Mrs Davies invited everyone to come up to the altar. Rees and Sara followed Tomos and Bethan. They moved slowly and reverently until it was their turn to kneel before the altar.

Mrs Davies placed a small piece of bread in Bethan's outstretched hands, saying 'The body of Christ'. Bethan replied 'Amen', before eating the bread. The reader gave the chalice to Bethan, saying 'The blood of Christ'. Bethan replied 'Amen', before sipping the wine. Mrs Davies placed her hand on Rees and Sara's bowed heads and blessed them. Rees and Sara felt very special.

Visiting the church with Bethan and Tomos had taught Rees and Sara a lot about their friends. They had learnt that Christians believe that it is important to worship God together as a community. A special part of this worship is the communion service where the community share together bread and wine.

6

2 Midnight mass at Christmas

It was the day before Christmas and Rees and Sara were growing more and more excited. When the post had arrived early that morning, even more Christmas cards had been delivered to their house. They knew that no more cards could come now, apart from the few stragglers that always arrived after Christmas. Uncle Randolph always posted his far too late.

So, Rees and Sara settled down to look through all the cards just one last time before arranging them for Christmas day. Some cards carried pictures of snow-covered houses, churches, and inns, all set in olden days. A few cards had robins, green holly with red berries, or festive candles. Many cards this year featured teddy bears, and some told the Christmas story.

The card from Bethan and Tomos was different from all the rest. The picture showed St David's Church decorated for Christmas. Inside the card, there was a list of the Christmas services.

Tonight the midnight mass was going to start at half past eleven and Rees and Sara were being allowed to go for the first time.

At eleven o'clock Rees and Sara wrapped up warm in their winter coats and waited excitedly for the door bell to ring. Bethan and Tomos were going to take them to the midnight mass. Rees and Sara had never stayed up so late on Christmas eve before.

Outside there was a deep chill in the air. A light coating of frost covered the cars. The Christmas lights sparkled and danced in the shop windows. Rees and Sara were startled by the bright sound of the church bells across the crisp night air. There were six bells in the tower at St David's.

Mr Davies explained, 'Each bell needs one person to ring it. So tonight you can hear all six bells being rung. It is called ringing the changes.' Rees and Sara stood still to listen.

When they got close to the church door, Rees and Sara could hear the choir leading the singing. As people walked in they were welcomed by the joyful sound of familiar Christmas carols. Rees and Sara knew some of the carols from school. They joined in the lullaby rhythm of 'Away in a manger', in the hushed tones of 'Silent night', and in the rousing chorus of 'Angels from the realms of glory'.

While some people went straight to their seats, others walked round the church to admire the Christmas decorations. There was a really large Christmas tree at the entrance to the Lady Chapel. Lots of presents had been placed round the tree. These presents would be shared among the children in the local hospital.

Rees and Sara looked at the Christmas story retold by pupils from local schools in huge murals around the church.

They saw the Angel Gabriel telling Mary that she would have a baby boy and name him Jesus.

They saw Mary and Joseph setting out on their long journey to Bethlehem where Jesus was born.

They saw the innkeeper leading Mary and Joseph to the stable, because the inn was already full.

They saw the infant Jesus placed in the animals' feeding trough as a make-shift cot, while the animals looked on.

They saw the angels call the shepherds away from their sheep to come to visit the baby Jesus.

They saw the wise men following the star to bring their gifts of gold, frankincense, and myrrh to the baby Jesus.

At half past eleven the service began. Mrs Davies wore a festive chasuble and she was led by the crucifier and the acolytes to the splendid Christmas crib at the front of the church. Mrs Davies blessed the crib and prayed the Christmas collect.

Eternal God,
who made this most holy night
to shine with the brightness of your one true light;
bring us, who have known the revelation of that light on earth,
to see the radiance of your heavenly glory;
through Jesus Christ, your Son our Lord.
Amen.

Then, the first communion service of Christmas was ready to begin.

After sharing midnight mass alongside their friends Bethan and Tomos, Rees and Sara felt that they understood better what Christmas really means to Christians today. The real meaning of Christmas is not to be found in the cards showing holly, robins, and snow-covered inns, but in the birth of Jesus.

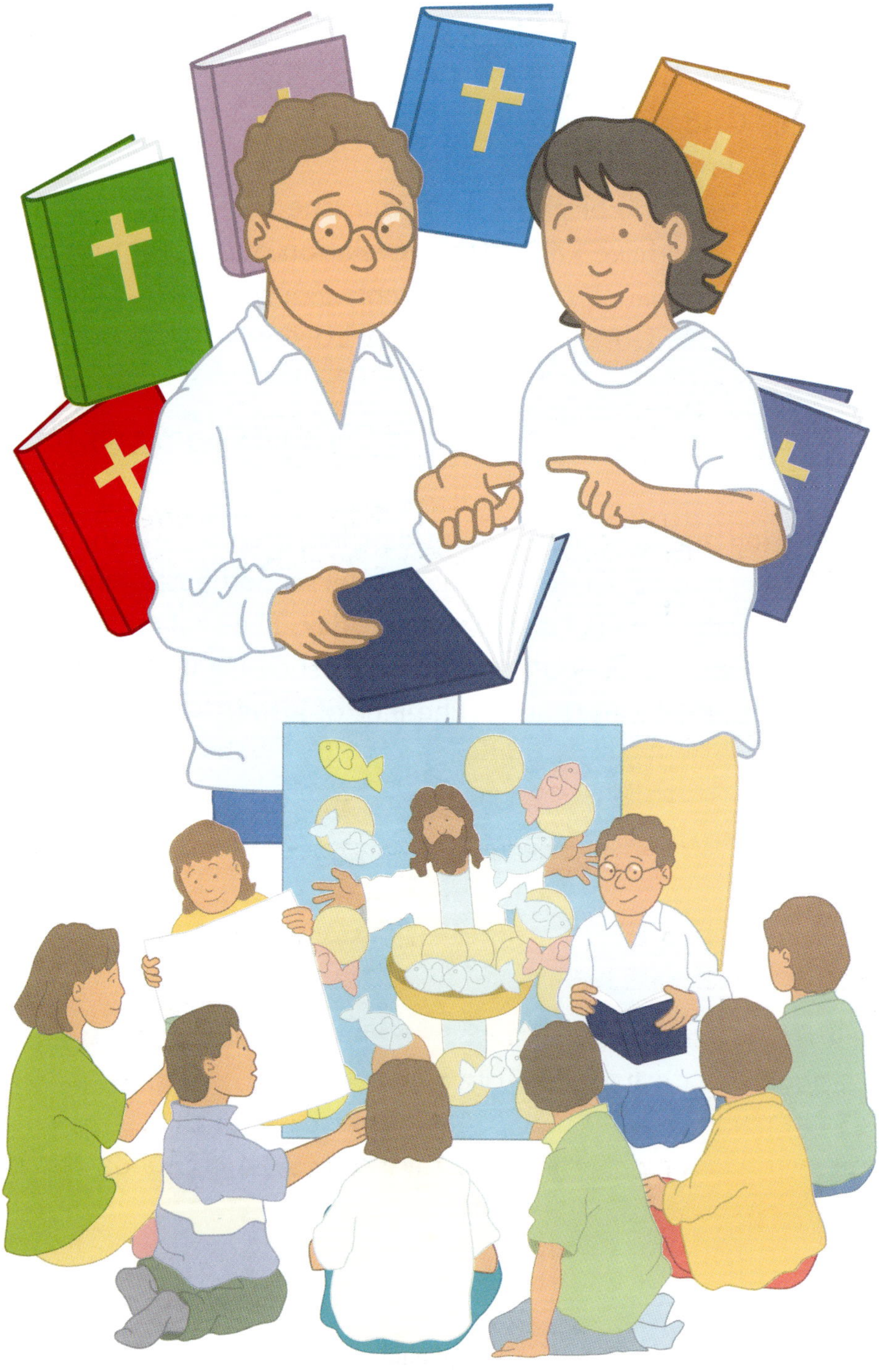

3 Using the Bible

On the day when Bethan and Tomos had received communion for the first time, Mr and Mrs Davies had given them each a copy of the Bible. They had written inside the message:

> You are a child of God
> supported by word and sacrament.

Weeks later, Rees and Sara found Tomos' Bible in his room. They read the message inside. Sara was puzzled and asked Tomos what it meant. Tomos thought for a moment and said, 'The word is the Bible. The sacrament is the bread and the wine. As Christians, we grow in our faith by reading God's word in the Bible and by receiving the sacrament of the bread and the wine.'

Rees and Sara opened Tomos' Bible and saw that there were two main sections inside. The first section is called the Old Testament and the second section is called the New Testament.

In the Old Testament there are 39 different books and in the New Testament, there are 27 books. Tomos said, 'The Bible is like a whole library of books with many different stories. The stories help us to understand God and to live good lives.'

On most Tuesday evenings eight or nine people came to Bethan and Tomos' house for a Bible Study Group. 'That is when the worship leaders meet to read the Bible and to get ready for the Sunday service,' said Bethan.

On most Thursdays after school the children from the church came round to Bethan and Tomos' house. 'The Thursday club is good fun,' said Tomos. 'We listen to a story from the Bible. Then we make a poster or a model to take to church on Sunday to teach the grown-ups about the story.'

Rees and Sara knew that the Bible was very important in Bethan and Tomos' church. Their teacher had taken them on a school trip to St David's Church.

On the trip, Rees and Sara had asked Mrs Davies about the large gleaming brass bird that stood at the front, wings outstretched. 'That', Mrs Davies had said, 'is the eagle. It carries the Bible on its wings to bring the word of God to the whole world. People stand behind the eagle to read aloud from the Bible in our service.'

Mrs Davies had explained to Rees and Sara that Christians read the Bible at home to learn about God. 'But what really makes the Bible come alive for me is how we use the Bible in our Sunday services. Why not come and see?'

On Sunday Rees and Sara went to the service with Tomos and Bethan. This time they wanted to see how the Bible was used in church.

In the service Rees and Sara saw a man walk up to the gleaming eagle. 'The first reading is from the Old Testament,' he said. Then at the end of the reading, he said, 'This is the Word of the Lord,' and everyone replied, 'Thanks be to God.'

Later in the service, Rees and Sara saw a woman walk up to the gleaming eagle. 'The second reading is from the New Testament,' she said. Then at the end of the reading, she said, 'This is the Word of the Lord,' and everyone replied, 'Thanks be to God.'

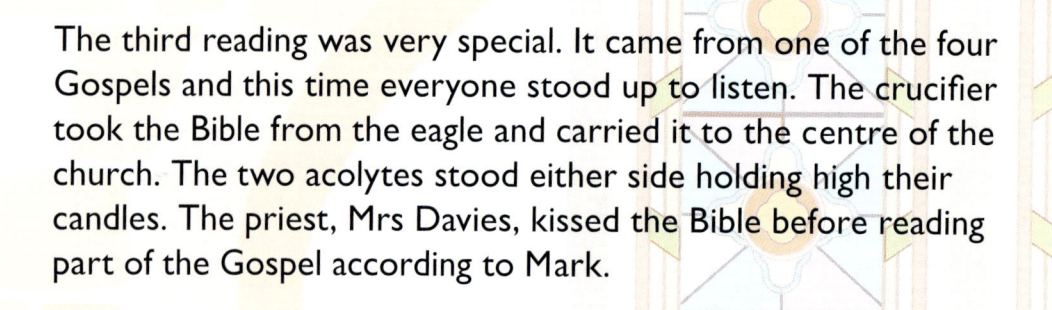

The third reading was very special. It came from one of the four Gospels and this time everyone stood up to listen. The crucifier took the Bible from the eagle and carried it to the centre of the church. The two acolytes stood either side holding high their candles. The priest, Mrs Davies, kissed the Bible before reading part of the Gospel according to Mark.

Rees and Sara went home from church knowing just how special the Bible was to their friends, Tomos and Bethan, and to all the people who worshipped in St David's Church. At home Christians study the Bible to learn about God and to live good lives. At church Christians read the Bible aloud to celebrate God's caring relationship with human beings, and to learn what God's word means for Christians today.

18

4 Christian Aid

Rees and Sara attended the same primary school as Bethan and Tomos. It was a large school with many different classes. The classes were taught by different teachers and usually the different year groups followed different lessons. Sometimes, however, the whole school worked on a special project.

In early September Mrs Williams visited the school. She came from the Development Education Centre and went round all the classes in turn. She helped the school to set up a special project on fairtrade.

Until the half term holiday each class worked hard to make a huge display in the school hall about fairtrade.

Mrs William's visit to the school was sponsored by Oxfam and by Christian Aid. Both Oxfam and Christian Aid do the same kind of work. They are both concerned with world development and work well together. But Christian Aid is different from Oxfam in one important way. Christian Aid was set up by the Christian Churches to respond to the Christian call to serve the poor of the world in the name of God.

Sara and Bethan's class explored the journey of a banana from growing on a tree to their local shop.

The journey begins with the hard work of the grower, far away in the Caribbean. A development company helps the grower to sell the bananas. A shipping, importing, and packaging company ensures that the bananas arrive safely in our country. A wholesaler buys the bananas and sells them to different retailers or shops.

The class was surprised to discover how little the growers are paid for their bananas. This means that they live in poverty. Many of the others involved in the banana's journey get paid a lot more. This means that they are much richer. The children thought that this was not fair.

Sara and Bethan's class made a poster showing what they had learnt about bananas. The poster was displayed in the school hall.

Rees and Tomos' class visited one of the local supermarkets to find out more about fairtrade products. Rees stood by the supermarket entrance and asked shoppers to complete a questionnaire on fairtrade. The questionnaire asked four questions.

Do you buy fairtrade products?
If you buy fairtrade products, which ones do you buy?
If you buy fairtrade products, why do you buy them?
If you do not buy fairtrade products, why do you not buy them?

Tomos interviewed the supermarket manager about fairtrade products in her supermarket. He made a list of all the fairtrade products the supermarket sold.

Back at school Rees and Tomos' class made a poster showing what they had learnt in the supermarket. The poster was displayed in the school hall.

When all the classes had finished their work, Mrs Williams came back to the school to share in a big celebration. Leaders from the local churches and faith groups came as well.

Children from every class told everyone what they had done and what they had learnt. Most children mentioned two important things. They believed that world trade is not fair because it is a cause of much poverty around the world. They had learnt that there are things which can be done to change this.

From now on the school staff room would only serve fairtrade tea and fairtrade coffee. From now on the school shop would only sell fairtrade bananas.

Mrs Davies was so impressed by the children's presentation she asked to take their display to St David's Church.

In the service on Sunday Mrs Davies spoke about the work of Christian Aid. She read from the Bible how Jesus taught his followers to treat others fairly. In Luke's Gospel, chapter 6, Jesus said,

> Give to everyone who asks you;
> if anyone takes what is yours, do not demand it back.
> Treat others as you would like them to treat you.
> If you love only those who love you,
> what credit is that to you?

Christian Aid, Mrs Davies said, was set up to carry out Jesus' teaching in the world today.

Like several other children from the school, Rees and Sara went to St David's Church to see their work displayed. Listening to Mrs Davies, they learnt how Christians are inspired by Jesus' teaching to treat others fairly.

24

5 Celebrating harvest

In late September the parish church celebrated Harvest Thanksgiving. Bethan and Tomos invited their friends Rees and Sara to join in.

On Saturday morning lots of Bethan and Tomos' friends met in the church hall for a project day. The theme was 'Bread and Wine'. During the day, there were many different workshops from which to choose.

In the morning Rees and Tomos joined a group visiting the local supermarket. They learned about all the different kinds of bread on display and bought some to bring back to church. There was a long baguette from France, ciabatta bread from Italy, and naan bread from India. When they came back to the hall, the group made a collage to hang on the altar. They called the collage 'Bread across the world'. Rees saw how bread united the peoples of the world.

In the morning Sara and Bethan joined a group visiting a farm. They learned about how flour was made. The story involved the sowing of the seed, the rain, the sun and the nutrients in the soil. The story involved the people who made the tractor, who harvested the grain, and who worked the mills to grind the flour. When they came back to the hall, the group prepared a dance to tell the story of flour. They called the dance 'Fruit of the earth and work of human hands'.

In the afternoon Rees and Tomos joined a group baking bread. The children who had visited the farm brought back a bag of grain. Rees ground the grain in a hand mill to turn it into flour.

Tomos mixed the flour with yeast and water to make dough. Then he kneaded it for a long time before watching it grow twice its size by the warmth of a radiator. The dough was used to make many interesting shapes. Some children made a special harvest loaf shaped like a sheaf of corn. Other children made little bread loaves which could be used in the harvest communion service.

Rees and Tomos saw how the bread used in the communion service symbolised all the fruits of the earth and work of human hands.

In the afternoon Sara and Bethan joined a group making wine. The previous day Mrs Davies had been out in the countryside picking ripe juicy blackberries. Sara washed the blackberries carefully.

Bethan weighed the blackberries on an old-fashioned set of scales. The children needed to add just the right amount of water, the right amount of sugar, and the right amount of yeast.

The mixture was poured into special glass bottles. A large cork and valve were placed in the top of the bottle. Then the valve was primed with water. As the fermentation began air bubbles escaped from the jar but no bacteria could find their way into the fermenting wine.

Sara and Bethan saw how the wine used in the communion service symbolised all the fruits of the earth and work of human hands.

Throughout Saturday some of the children helped the adults to decorate St David's Church for the Sunday service. For the harvest festival, the church was full of the fruits of the earth. Around the font there were potatoes, carrots, parsnips, and leeks. In front of the altar there were tins of pears, peaches, grapefruit, and pineapples. There were ripe apples and golden pears.

For the harvest festival the church was full of the work of human hands. In the Lady Chapel local farmers had brought spades, hoes, and scythes from bygone days. They had brought the ploughs and spraying equipment used on farms today.

On Sunday the children hung their collage on the altar and they performed their dance about the story of flour.

When the altar was being prepared for communion, Tomos and Rees carried the bread which they had made. Bethan and Sara carried the large jar of fermenting wine. Mrs Davies received their gifts and gave thanks to God for the fruits of the earth and for the work of human hands.

In the harvest festival Rees and Sara had learnt much more about the people who worship in the parish church. They now understood how Christians depend on God for the fruits of the earth. They had learnt also how Christians cooperate with God through the work of human hands.

As Rees and Sara walked home, they agreed that they wanted to share some of their own special things with Tomos and Bethan. What these things are is another story.

In the World Faiths Today Series Rees and Sara learn about the major world faiths in their own country. The seven stories in the series are:

- Exploring Islam
- Exploring Judaism
- Exploring the Parish Church
- Exploring the Orthodox Church
- Exploring Hinduism
- Exploring Buddhism
- Exploring Sikhism

Welsh National Centre for Religious Education
Bangor University
Bangor
Gwynedd
Wales

© Welsh National Centre for Religious Education, 2008.

All rights reserved. These materials are subject to copyright and may not be reproduced or published without the permission of the copyright owner.

First published 2008.

Sponsored by the Welsh Assembly Government.

British Library Cataloguing-in-Publication Data
A catalogue record for this book is available from the British Library.

ISBN 978-1-85357-182-4

Printed and bound in Wales by Gwasg Dwyfor.